RACING CARS

This edition produced in **1993** for
Shooting Star Press Inc
230 Fifth Avenue
New York, NY 10001

Design David West
Children's Book Design

Editorial Lionheart Books

Researcher Cecilia Weston-Baker

Illustrator Ron Hayward Associates

Created and produced by
Aladdin Books Ltd
28 Percy Street
London W1P 9FF

*First published in the
United States in 1990 by*
Gloucester Press

ISBN 1-56924-011-6

Printed in Belgium

CONTENTS

HOW · IT · WORKS
RACING CARS

IAN GRAHAM

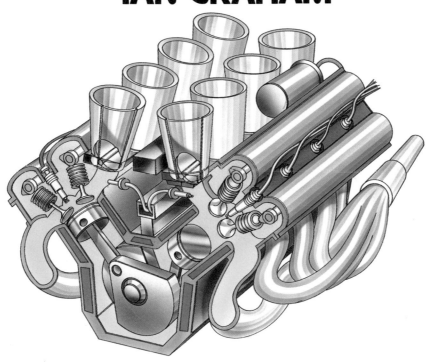

SHOOTING STAR PRESS

THE WORKING PARTS

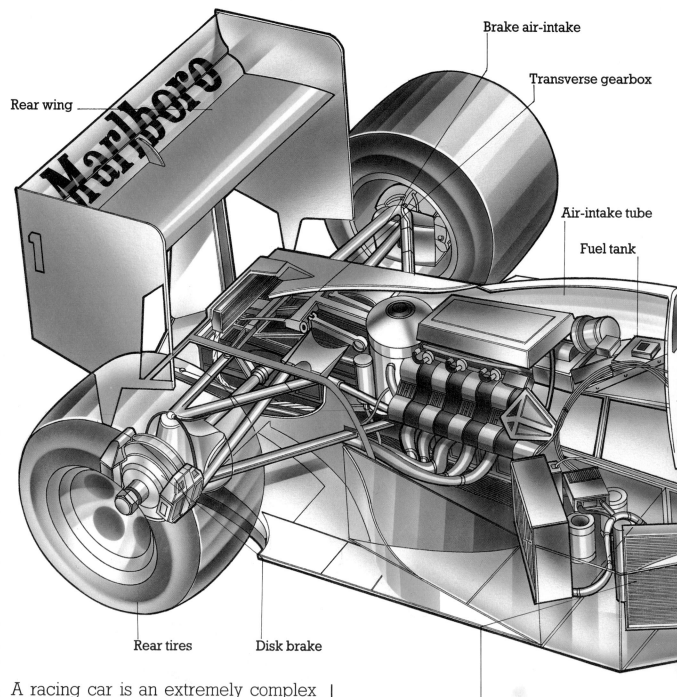

Rear wing

Brake air-intake

Transverse gearbox

Air-intake tube

Fuel tank

Rear tires

Disk brake

Water radiators

A racing car is an extremely complex vehicle designed to be driven safely at very high speeds. The "Grand Prix" cars that compete in the famous Formula 1 championship every year can reach speeds of up to 200 mph on specially designed racetracks. Car constructors use all the most modern materials, electronics and body designs to produce very strong and powerful cars that are also lightweight. The car is built around its power unit, the engine. Single-seat racing cars normally have the engine positioned at the rear of the vehicle, turning the rear wheels around. The driver sits in front of the engine inside a specially strengthened box designed to protect his or her body against the impact of a crash.

4

The shape of the car's body is very important. The car is always shaped "aerodynamically," with smooth curving panels to enable it to slip through the air easily. By positioning the wheels out to the side of the vehicle instead of underneath it, the car body can be lowered closer to the ground. This also helps to streamline the car and reduce the air resistance (drag) that acts against it to slow it down.

Small wings, or spoilers, at the front and rear of the car act like upside-down aircraft wings. As the car moves forward and air flows over these, they produce a down-force that pushes the vehicle down onto the track surface. This enables the car to go around corners at higher speeds without skidding.

Although most racing cars look considerably different from normal mass production family cars, a degree of the advanced technology developed for racing cars is later built into the cars that are offered for sale to the public.

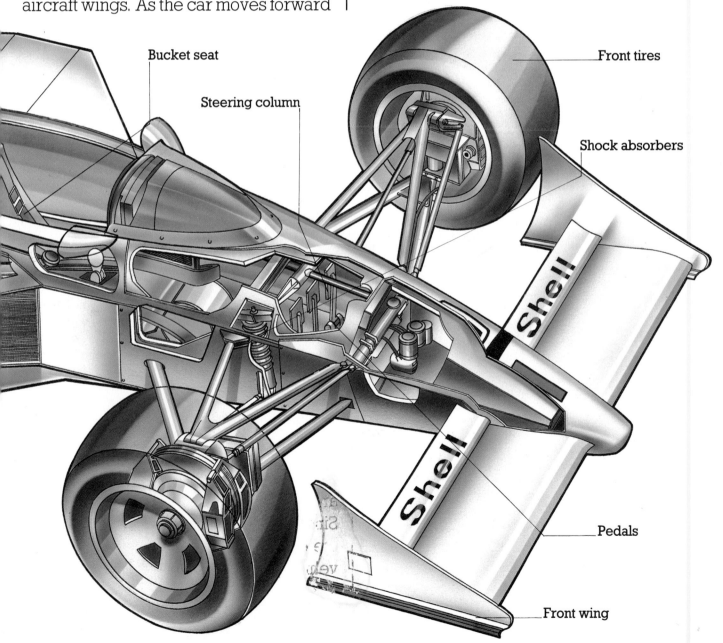

Bucket seat

Steering column

Front tires

Shock absorbers

Shell

Shell

Pedals

Front wing

DIFFERENT TYPES

The earliest motor races involved ordinary road cars, but the cars' owners and makers soon found ways of improving their vehicles' performance for racing. They modified the cars to suit the conditions of the race. Different types of races – over rough countryside, on smooth tracks or on ice – led to different types of racing cars. Modern cars designed for motor sports have become very specialized. Rally cars are designed for speed and endurance over long, winding courses on a variety of roads and loose surfaces. The annual 24-hour race at Le Mans in France involves very powerful sports cars that can travel at over 200 mph.

Single-seat racing cars are divided into several "formulas." Each formula is controlled by strict rules on engine size, car size and weight, and design features. By far the most popular is Formula 1. Others include Formula 2 and Formula 3000. Drag racers are designed to travel as fast as possible over very short, straight courses. Trucks are raced too, and so are some ordinary production cars.

A rally car in action. It is a modified, high-performance production car.

A single-seat racing car.

There are even races for production cars.

Not all races involve specialized "Formula" cars. This is an aerodynamic Le Mans sports car.

CREATING THE POWER

A Grand Prix car engine works in the same way as a normal car engine. A mixture of fuel (gasoline) and air is sprayed into each of the cylinders, compressed by a piston and ignited by an electric spark. The fuel/air mixture explodes and forces the piston down. The other end of the piston is connected to a shaft which rotates and, through a series of mechanical linkages, drives the car's wheels. The movements of a number of pistons are timed to produce a series of these "power strokes" one after another. This happens so rapidly that the wheels are driven around smoothly. The size of the cylinders is

V8 Four-stroke engine

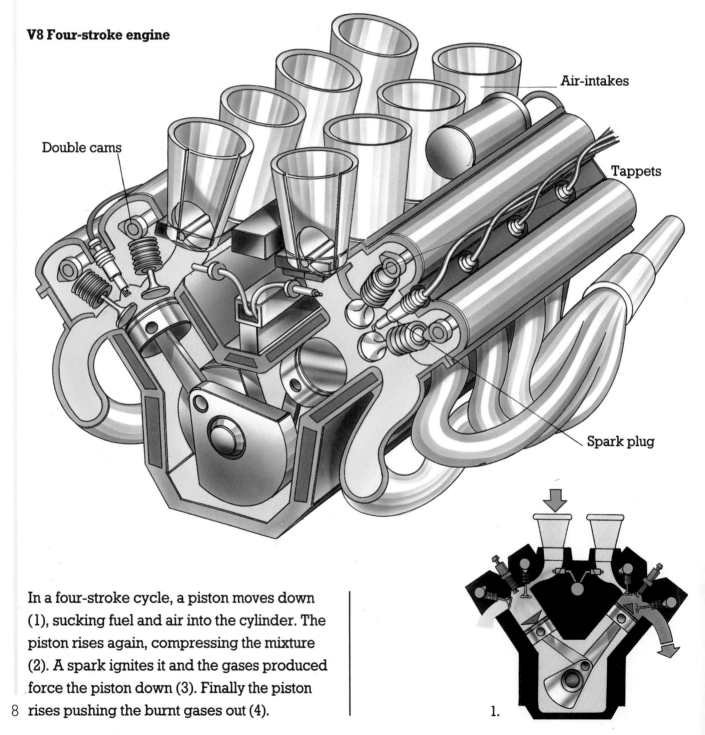

Double cams

Air-intakes

Tappets

Spark plug

In a four-stroke cycle, a piston moves down (1), sucking fuel and air into the cylinder. The piston rises again, compressing the mixture (2). A spark ignites it and the gases produced force the piston down (3). Finally the piston rises pushing the burnt gases out (4).

1.

limited by the rules of the sport. For example, from 1989 Formula 1 cars have a total cylinder capacity of 3.5 liters.

The majority of Grand Prix cars are powered by the Ford Cosworth V8 engine. It is called a V8 engine because it has eight cylinders in two banks of four set at an angle to each other forming a V shape. The Cosworth engine was developed in the 1960s and updated versions are still in use. A new model was developed for the 1988 racing season. Grand Prix car engines are also made by Ferrari, Honda, Lamborghini, Judd, Renault and Yamaha, with 8, 10 or 12 cylinders.

A Formula 1 V10 engine.

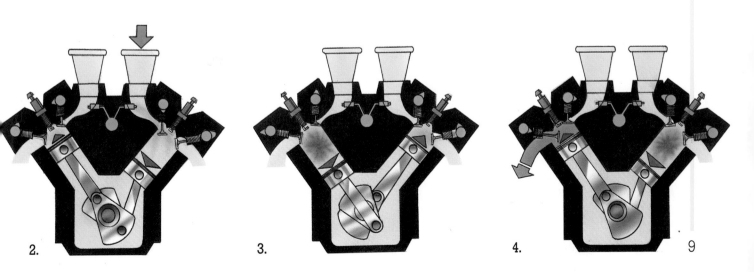

2.   3.   4.

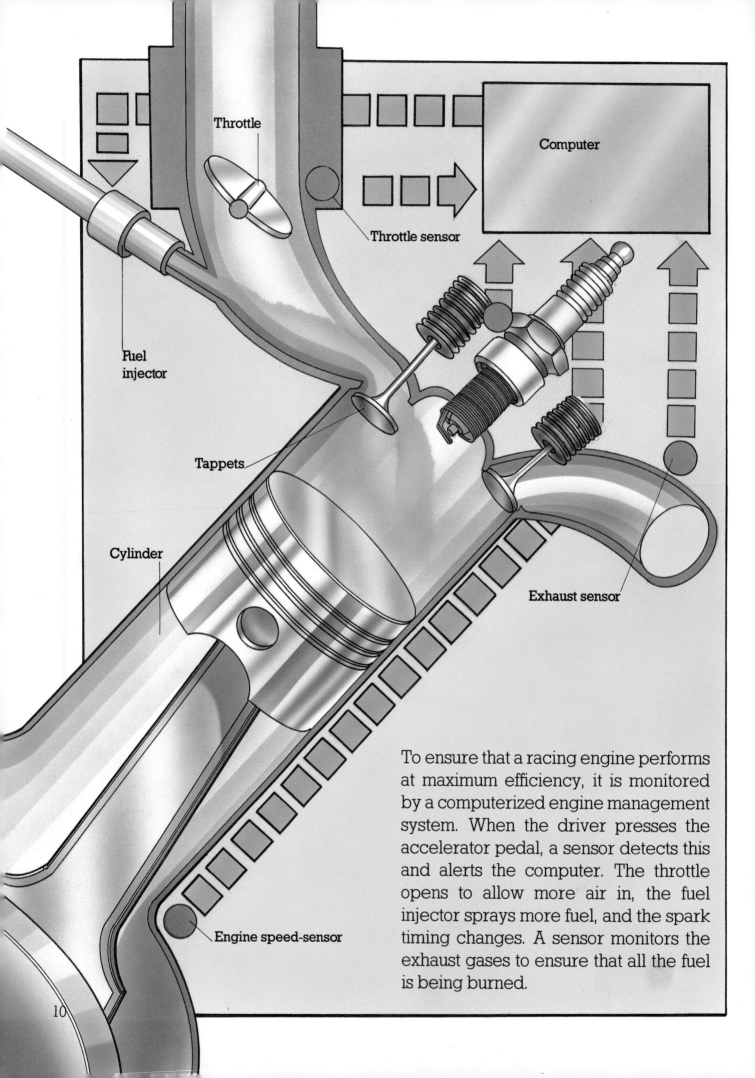

Throttle

Computer

Throttle sensor

Fuel
injector

Tappets

Cylinder

Exhaust sensor

Engine speed-sensor

To ensure that a racing engine performs at maximum efficiency, it is monitored by a computerized engine management system. When the driver presses the accelerator pedal, a sensor detects this and alerts the computer. The throttle opens to allow more air in, the fuel injector sprays more fuel, and the spark timing changes. A sensor monitors the exhaust gases to ensure that all the fuel is being burned.

INCREASING THE POWER

Engine power can be increased by boosting the pressure of the fuel-air mixture that is burned inside the engine. This was realized as early as 1923, when the "supercharger" was introduced. The first supercharger was an air pump driven by the engine. It blew air into the engine's cylinders at high pressure. By the end of the 1930s, racing cars fitted with superchargers could travel at well over 186 mph. Superchargers were not readily available throughout World War II (1939-1945). They were not reintroduced to motor racing until 1977, and then under a new name – turbochargers. A turbocharger works using the force of the jet of exhaust gases pumped out by the engine. It increases engine pressure from atmospheric pressure, also called 1 bar, to the pressure allowed by the sport's rules. In 1987, Formula 1 engine pressure was limited to 4 bar (four times atmospheric pressure) and reduced to 2.5 bar in 1988. From 1989, turbocharged engines were banned from Formula 1 racing, but they are still used in numerous other motor sports.

A turbocharger is powered by energy that would otherwise be wasted. A propeller-like turbine in the exhaust pipe is rotated at high speed by hot exhaust gases rushing out of the engine. A shaft connects it to another turbine, called a compressor, positioned in the engine's air-intake. The exhaust turbine forces around the compressor, which increases the pressure of the air entering the engine. This results in greater engine power and also, surprisingly, a saving in fuel.

Drag racers use turbocharged engines for the maximum power and rate of acceleration along a short straight course. They have enormous rear tires to give the maximum grip on the track.

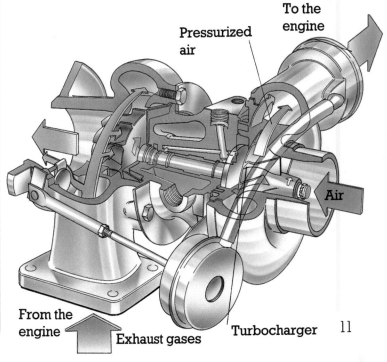

Pressurized air

To the engine

Air

From the engine

Exhaust gases

Turbocharger

POWER TO THE WHEELS

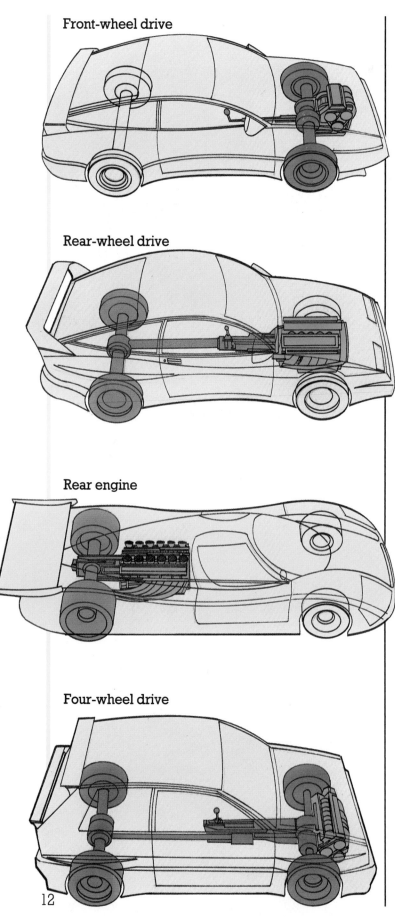

Front-wheel drive

Rear-wheel drive

Rear engine

Four-wheel drive

When a family car's engine is "on" but the accelerator pedal is not pressed, the crankshaft turns at about 750 rpm (revolutions per minute). If the shaft were connected directly to the wheels, this would make the car travel at about 50 mph – it would be impossible to control. In fact, a series of interlinked gear wheels reduces the speed of the crankshaft until the output shaft matches the required speed of the wheels. The gear wheels are contained in the gearbox. The correct gear wheels are linked together by positioning a selector called a gear lever. To change gear, the engine is first disconnected from the gearbox by pressing the "clutch" pedal. The gear lever is moved to the required position and then the clutch pedal is released to reconnect the engine. Some cars have an automatic transmission; they do not have a gear lever or clutch pedal. The gearbox automatically selects the correct gear for the car's speed.

Single-seat racing cars and some specialized sports cars have the engine mounted behind the driver. In this position, the engine's weight is over the wheels it drives, increasing tire grip. It also allows the front of the car to be made lower and thinner to reduce air resistance. Most mass production cars – station wagons, vans, jeeps and popular sports cars – have front engines, driving either the front wheels, the rear wheels or all four for maximum grip. Most front-mounted engines are placed lengthwise in the cars, but some are placed across (transverse engine).

Rally car drivers change gear thousands of times during a rally.

A gearbox contains two sets of gear wheels. The input and output shafts are on top, and the "layshaft" is underneath. When the gear lever is moved, selector rods push certain gear wheels together. If reverse gear is selected, an "idler" wheel slides between the layshaft and output shaft to reverse the direction of spin of the output.

Third-gear mode

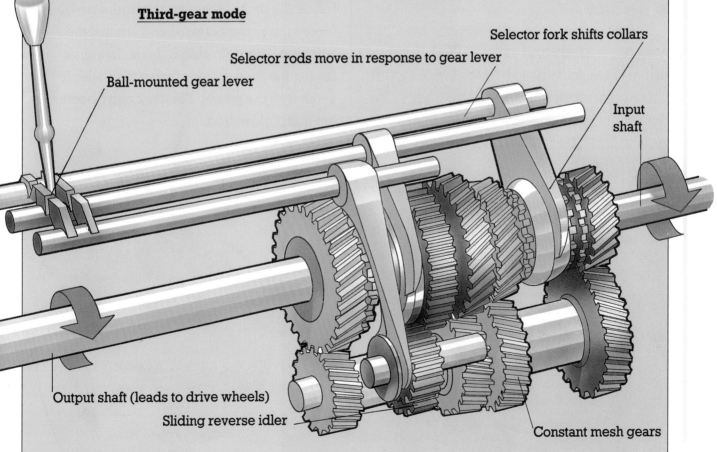

Selector fork shifts collars

Selector rods move in response to gear lever

Ball-mounted gear lever

Input shaft

Output shaft (leads to drive wheels)

Sliding reverse idler

Constant mesh gears

WHEELS

Racing-car wheels developed from the wheels of horsedrawn carriages. The wooden wheels were not strong enough for the powerful racing engines that were developed and they often broke. Solid metal wheels were strong enough, but too heavy. Wheels made from steel rims and hubs, linked by wire spokes (to save weight) were tried, but they were easily damaged. Eventually solid wheels made from lightweight alloys (mixtures of different metals) were developed and they are still used today. The wheels are fitted with tires made from a mixture of different rubbers, called the tire compound. Different compounds behave in different ways. Some compounds give better grip on wet surfaces. Others are more suitable for dry weather.

There are two types of braking systems – disk and drum. Disk brakes were developed for use by aircraft. They were first used in motor racing by Jaguar in the 1953 Le Mans sports car race in France. All racing cars now use disk brakes.

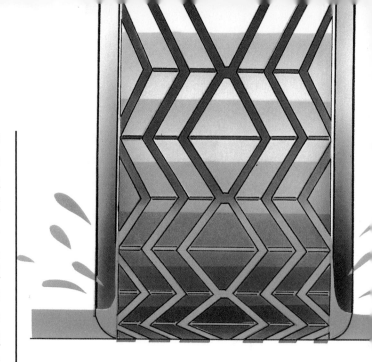

Wets

The tread pattern on rain tires, also called wets, forces water out from beneath the tire and keeps the maximum area of rubber in contact with the track.

In a drum brake, a rough lining material is fixed to the surface of two curved "shoes" inside the drum. Pressing the brake pedal forces the shoes outward and against the spinning drum, slowing it down. In a disk brake, flat friction pads grip a disk which spins with the wheel. The disk can become so hot that it glows red.

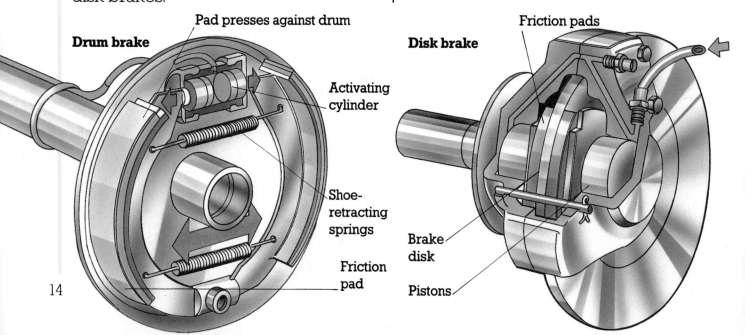

Drum brake

Pad presses against drum

Activating cylinder

Shoe-retracting springs

Friction pad

Disk brake

Friction pads

Brake disk

Pistons

Slicks

In dry weather a tread pattern is not necessary. Dry-weather tires, called slicks, are smooth and made from a soft rubber that is sticky when warm, to give maximum grip.

Snow tires

Rally cars often have to be driven over snow or ice-covered roads and tracks. To give them some grip on these slippery surfaces, they may use tires with metal studs.

Rain tires gripping a wet track in spectacular fashion.

SUSPENSION

If a car were connected to its wheels by rigid shafts and struts, it would be uncontrollable at high speed. The whole car would vibrate and jump as the wheels bounced over every little bump in the road surface. Every racing car is therefore linked to its wheels through a system of levers, springs and pistons called its suspension system. This allows the wheels to bounce over bumps without the rest of the car doing the same. The suspension system is said to absorb or damp unwanted movements.

In the 1970s the Lotus Formula 1 racing team began to develop a completely new type of suspension system. A car's aerodynamics works at its best if the car body can be kept at a constant height from the track surface. Normal suspension systems cannot achieve this. If the driver brakes hard, the car's nose dips down. When the car goes around a corner, it rolls toward the outside of the corner. And when it accelerates, the nose comes up and the rear of the car dips down. All these changes in position upset the car's aerodynamics. The active suspension system developed by Lotus used fast-acting jacks controlled by a computer to raise or lower each corner of the car when necessary, so that the body remained level at all times.

The size of the wheels is important, too, for smooth traveling. Racing cars have larger wheels than production cars.

In some motor sports on rough ground, suspension systems must be very strong indeed!

A shock absorber consists of a piston with a spring coiled around it. When a wheel goes over a bump, the pushrod is forced upward. The spring is compressed and then released. The oil-filled piston prevents the spring from bouncing up and down. It "damps" the spring.

Fluid feed and return pipe

Piston

Coil spring

Push rod

Push rod pivot

An active suspension system keeps a car level, at a constant "ride height," by replacing the normal coil springs and dampers with computer controlled jacks. If the car's nose tries to dip, sensors detect the movement and alert the computer. In a fraction of a second, the computer calculates the action necessary to counteract this unwanted movement and instructs the front jacks to raise the nose.

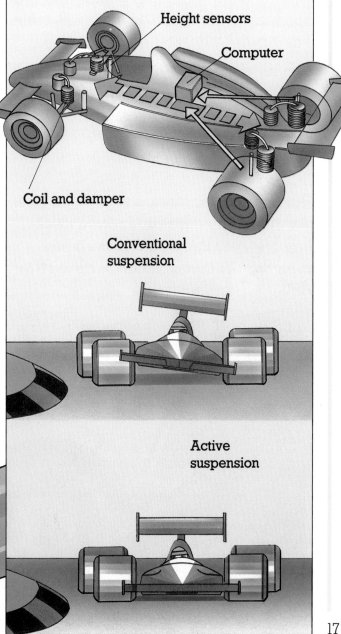

Height sensors

Computer

Coil and damper

Conventional suspension

Active suspension

AERODYNAMICS

The way that air flows around a car creates forces which affect the car's speed and performance. The study of airflow around objects is called aerodynamics. Racing car designers make their cars low and slim with a smooth curving shape to keep air resistance to a minimum. In the late 1960s, designers all began to use aerodynamics to improve racing car performance. The first development was the nose winglet. A pair of wings, or spoilers, were fixed to the car's nose. They behaved like upside-down wings and helped to force the front of the car down onto the track. A rear wing, running the full width of the car, was added to hold the rear of the car down at high speed.

Grand Prix racing cars and some sports cars use wings to produce a down-force which improves road holding and allows faster cornering. Air flowing under the curved front

Designers then examined how to use the shape of the car itself to improve its performance. By using "side skirts" extending down to the ground and by shaping the bottom of the car, the air pressure underneath the whole car could be reduced to create more down-force. A good number of these developments, including moving wings and underbody shaping, were banned within a year or two when the rules governing Formula 1 car design were changed by the sport's authorities.

To develop a new racing car shape, designers make scale models of the car and test them in "wind tunnels." Here they study the flow of air over the bodywork using cameras and computers.

and rear wings travels further than the air flowing over the flatter top surface. This creates a difference in air pressure above and below the wings and causes the down-force.

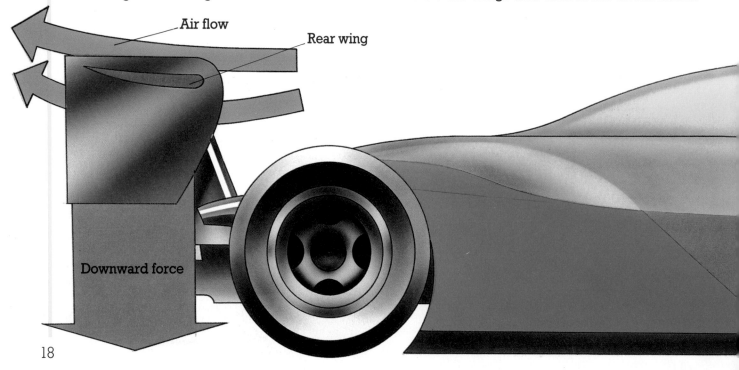

Air flow

Rear wing

Downward force

 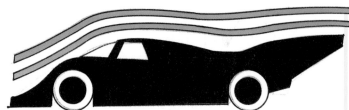

The angular shape of most family cars causes turbulence in the air flowing over the car, particularly at the rear end.

Racing cars are shaped to allow air to flow over them smoothly without causing any turbulence.

Turbulent "vortexes" of air spiral away from the rear wing of a Formula 1 car.

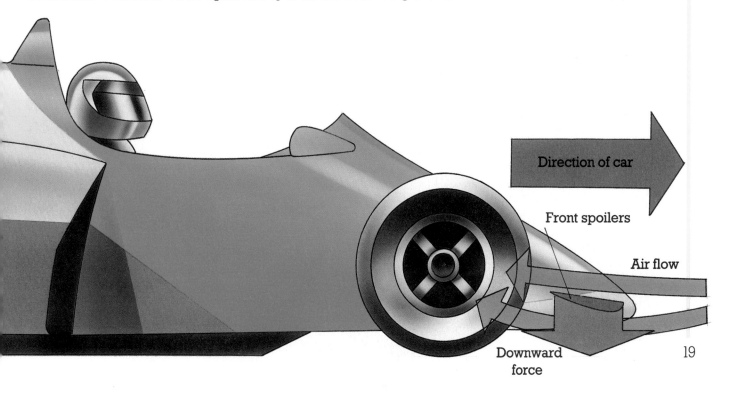

Direction of car

Front spoilers

Air flow

Downward force

BEHIND THE WHEEL

Driving a racing car is very difficult and tiring. Cornering at high speed creates forces on the driver which can double or triple his weight. A driver's head and helmet normally weigh about 15lbs, but during a race his neck muscles may have to cope with more than double that as the car weaves in and out of corners.

Rapid acceleration and braking also throw the driver's head backward and forward. Racing car drivers must be very fit to withstand these forces.

To keep the car as low on the road as possible, the driver lies on his back in a seat specially shaped to fit the shape of the driver's body. The seat's close fit

The view inside driver Nigel Mansell's Formula 1 Ferrari racing car.

helps to spread the effects of cornering and great accelerating forces more comfortably over the whole body.

There are few instruments on the dashboard in front of the driver, because there is little time to look down at them during a race. The most important controls – steering wheel, gear lever and foot pedals – are similar to those in a normal production car. The instruments show fuel and oil pressure, oil temperature and water temperature. The largest instrument is usually the rev counter which shows engine speed. The driver uses this and engine noise to decide when to change gear.

The dashboard of a modern racing car.

A racing car's steering wheel (1) is smaller than in a normal car. Dials and indicators on the dashboard (2) give important information about the engine. The driver's feet operate three pedals. The clutch (3) disconnects the engine from the wheels during gear changes. The brakes (4) slow the car down when necessary. The accelerator or throttle pedal (5) is pressed to make the car go faster. To the driver's right, a short gear lever (6) is used to select the correct gear to match the engine's speed with the car's speed. The specially shaped seat (7) holds the driver firmly in the right position. In Formula 1 racing cars especially, the driver lies, rather than sits, in position, with arms and legs outstretched. A harness holds him in securely.

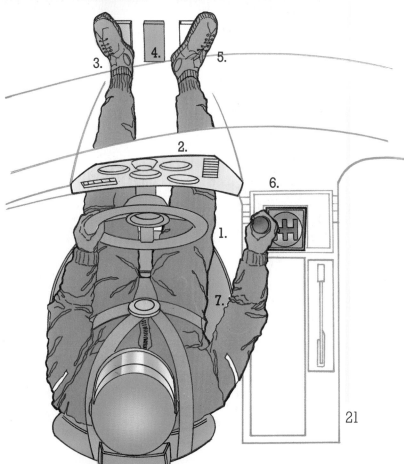

21

SAFETY

Racing drivers are protected from accidents and injuries in three ways – by safe car construction methods, by protective clothing and by emergency systems built into the car. The box inside which the driver sits is built to survive the most serious crash and the driver is strapped into it very tightly by a special harness.

Racing drivers wear a fireproof suit with close-fitting gloves and lightweight boots. The driver's head is protected by a strong lightweight crash helmet. If a driver is trapped in a burning car, the fireproof suit will protect him or her until fire-fighters reach the car. But the driver could be starved of oxygen as it is used up by the fire, or breathe in hot poisonous smoke. Grand Prix cars are fitted with a small oxygen tank connected to the driver's helmet by a tube so that the person can continue breathing. Small fires can be put out by the car's own extinguisher.

A nasty crash, or pile-up, at the 1989 Formula 1 French Grand Prix.

Every inch of a racing driver's body is covered by protective materials. The only visible area of skin is a slit across the eyes. This is protected by a clear visor that is capable of withstanding a shotgun blast. If the car should roll upside down, roll bars over the driver's knees and behind his head stop it from collapsing on him. The cockpit is such a tight fit that the driver can only get in and out of the car by removing the steering wheel. It is designed to come away very quickly in an emergency.

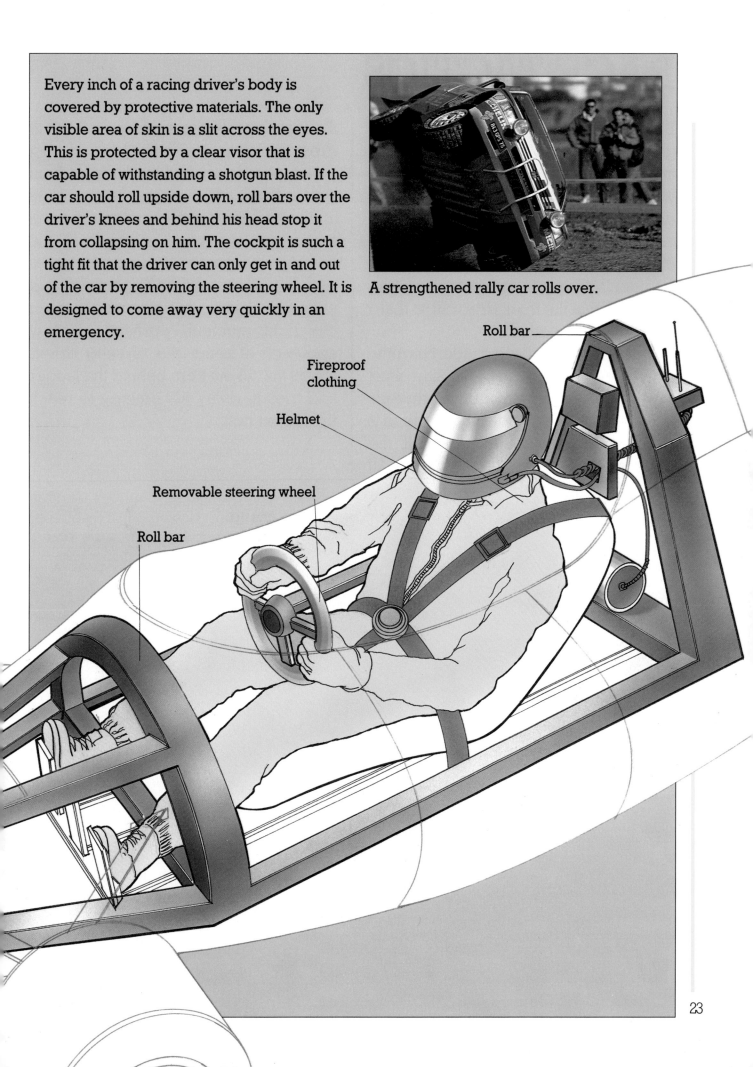

A strengthened rally car rolls over.

Roll bar

Fireproof clothing

Helmet

Removable steering wheel

Roll bar

RACE TACTICS

Before a race, teams plan what they are going to do during the event – their race tactics. If the track is wet, some may start with wet-weather tires on the car and change to dry-weather "slick" tires later on. Pit teams practice until they can change all four wheels in about eight seconds! Other teams may start on slicks and hope that the track dries out so that a pit stop is not needed.

The start of a race is a dangerous time. Any driver who is unable to start must raise his hand to warn other drivers. When the starter decides that the time is right, he switches lights that all the drivers can see from red to green. All the cars accelerate rapidly and try to slip past slower cars in front.

Unless a driver can lead a race from start to finish, which is rare, he must pass all the cars in front of his to win. As one car nears the rear of another, the aerodynamics of the leading car causes a suction effect called a "slipstream" that pulls the chasing car along behind. At the right moment, perhaps as they approach a bend, the chasing driver steers his car out from behind the leader and tries to delay his braking to reach the corner first.

Every driver is eager to get a fast start at this Formula 1 race line up.

Drivers must choose the right moment carefully to overtake cars in front.

Pit mechanics practice their work to make pit stops as short as possible.

Colored flags are used to send messages to drivers. If the race has to be stopped, a red flag is waved. A yellow flag warns drivers not to overtake cars in front. A blue flag shows a driver that a car is closing fast from behind. The checkered flag marks the end of the race. With many cars on the track, lights, not a person with a flag, start a race.

Stop the race

No overtaking

Car behind

End of race

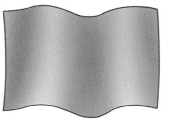

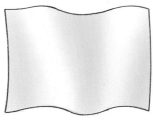

SPECIALS

Motor sport comes in many different forms. Formula 1 and sports car racing are only a small part of it. Other forms of motor sport include karting, truck racing, truck pulls and drag racing. Each requires its own type of vehicle specially designed for that particular activity.

Many of these different forms of motor sports are divided into their own specialist classes. Go-karts, for example, are subdivided into a variety of different classes. They range from "Cadet" karts, designed to introduce youngsters to the sport, up to more powerful Superkarts that are capable of speeds of up to 155 mph.

In truck racing, the cab units that normally pull freight containers are raced against each other around a track. Drag racing involves cars with very powerful turbocharged engines and enormous rear wheels to grip the track. The drag racers, or dragsters, normally race two at a time down a short course, also known as a strip. Some of these powerful cars are used in truck pulls, where they try to drag a heavy load over a set distance in the shortest time. As with all racing cars, they are very noisy!

The Paris-Dakar car rally is one of the toughest rallies in the world. The cars are driven from Paris, France, across the Sahara to Dakar in Senegal, West Africa.

One of the least expensive forms of motor racing, and therefore one of the easiest to take part in, is go-karting. The karts are very simple mechanically yet they provide fast races.

Drag racers are specially designed to accelerate down a 0.2 mile track as fast as possible. The cars can reach 250 mph in less than 6 seconds. They usually have incredibly large, wide wheels.

Stock cars are allowed to bump into each other as they overtake each other. They are therefore built very strongly to withstand the knocks. Often, many of the cars are too damaged to finish the race.

HISTORY OF THE RACING CAR

The first motor races were held in France in the 1890s. Only the car makers and a few wealthy car owners had enough time and money to take part. Each car carried a driver and a mechanic. The cars were so unreliable that the mechanics often had to repair their cars during a race. Neither the driver nor the mechanic wore a crash helmet or a seat belt.

One of the first motor races in the 1890s.

In 1906, rules were drawn up by the sport's authorities to control the design of cars that could enter races and to control the races themselves. This special "formula" later became known as Formula 1. The cars were huge and very powerful. They could weigh up to one ton and be powered by engines of 10 liters or more at over 90 mph. One of their cylinders was as big as the whole engine of a modern production car. Their tires, steering and brakes were not good enough to cope with these speeds and engine power and so there were many accidents.

Supercharged car racing in the 1950s.

Bigger and more powerful racing cars were continually developed. The introduction of the supercharger in 1923 boosted engine power even more. The sport's authorities agreed that the rapid increase in engine power had reached dangerous levels. In 1934, they made new rules limiting the weight of a racing car to 1,650lbs in an attempt to prevent top speeds from rising any further. Manufacturers overcame these rules by building cars from very light materials and using new mixtures of fuels to create more power. The most powerful car of the time was the Mercedes W125. In 1937, this managed to reach almost 200mph.

The Lotus 25 introduced the monocoque.

In 1958, the Cooper Car Company turned a car back to front and put the engine behind the driver. Others had done it before, but Cooper was the first to win Grand Prix races with rear-engined cars. Other manufacturers copied them. In 1962, Colin Chapman's Lotus team introduced the monocoque, meaning single shell. It replaced the car's basic framework or "chassis" with a single strong yet lightweight structure. Everyone copied this.

The latest type of Formula 1 racing car.

Car aerodynamics developed rapidly during the 1970s. In 1977, Lotus introduced the ground effect car, which used the car's shape to create a down-force. Also in 1977, Renault introduced a new engine to challenge the 3-liter Ford-Cosworth engine. It was half the size of the Cosworth, but turbocharged. At first it was not reliable, but quickly improved. More teams began to use them. By the late 1980s, the sport's authorities felt that the engines were too powerful and costly. From the 1989 racing season, turbochargers were banned.

FACTS AND FIGURES

The first motor race was held on June 11-13, 1887 in France, from Paris to Bordeaux and back, a distance of 730 miles. The winner, Emile Levassor, traveled at an average speed of 15 mph.

The world's largest sporting event is Indianapolis 500 motor race, with a race-day crowd of over 300,000 people.

The Monaco Grand Prix, driven on the roads of Monte Carlo, is thought to be the toughest Grand Prix circuit. During the 160 mile race, drivers have to change gear about 1,600 times.

The first motor race on a circuit was held on the Circuit du Sud-Ouest at Pau, France, in 1900.

A car driven by Bobby Unser was refueled in only four seconds during the 1976 Indianapolis 500 race – the fastest pit stop on record.

Over 2.5 million people attend the 16 Formula races held around the world, an average of over 150,000 spectators per race.

Between February 1961 and June 1964, Stan Mott of New York, drove his go-kart around the world, a distance of 23,000 miles on land through 28 countries.

GLOSSARY

active suspension
A computer controlled system that keeps a car at a fixed height above the ground.

CAD
Computer Aided Design. A computerized system used to help design cars.

carbon fiber
A black silky thread of pure carbon. The fibers can be woven together or mixed with other materials and set hard in a glue-like "resin" to form a very strong lightweight material.

CART
Championship Auto Racing Teams. A series of 17 races in the United States. The most famous is the 800km- (500 mile-) Indianapolis 500.

chassis
A car's basic frame, to which the engine, wheels and body are attached.

chicane
A corner or a series of barriers added to an existing track to reduce the cars' speed.

cockpit
The compartment in a racing car where the driver sits.

crankshaft
A rod or shaft which changes the up and down motion of the pistons in an engine into a turning motion to drive the wheels.

drag
A force that resists the movement of an object such as a car through air and tries to slow it down. Drag is reduced by streamlining a car.

engine management system
A computer control system which monitors the engine and sets its electrical timing.

FISA
Fédération Internationale du Sport Automobile. Motor sport's international governing organization.

fuel cell
A fuel tank containing a spongy material to soak up fuel and stop it from spilling out of a hole after an accident to reduce the risk of fire.

grand prix
Any of the 16 races that count toward the Formula 1 drivers' world championship. Grand prix is French for big prize.

lap
One circuit of a racetrack.

monocoque
A one piece chassis, sometimes called a bathtub or just a tub.

pits
A row of garages along a road called the pit lane which is positioned beside a racetrack's start-finish line. Cars enter the pits to refuel or for a tire change.

pole position

The leading position on the starting grid at the beginning of a race. The car that sets the fastest "qualifying lap" before the race starts the race in pole position.

production cars

Ordinary road cars produced in great numbers for sale to the general public, for example station wagons.

qualifier

A tire with a very soft rubber compound, used for maximum grip on qualifying laps. The soft compound may only last for three laps and cannot be used for the race itself.

rain tires

Tires made from a rubber compound designed to give good grip on a wet track. The "tread" of grooves cut in them lets water escape quickly from beneath them. Also called "wets."

slicks

Smooth tires made from a rubber compound that gives good grip on a dry track. The compound works best when the tire is at 140-212° Farenheit.

streamlining

Smoothing the shape of an object like a car, so that air flows over it with little or no turbulence.

turbocharger

A pump driven by the engine's exhaust for increasing the air pressure inside the engine to make it more powerful.

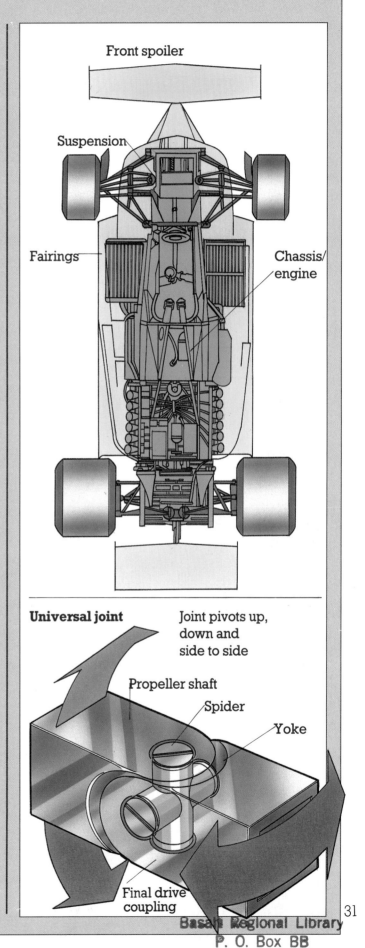

Front spoiler

Suspension

Fairings

Chassis/engine

Universal joint

Joint pivots up, down and side to side

Propeller shaft

Spider

Yoke

Final drive coupling

31

INDEX

Photographic credits
Cover and pages 20 and 24: Nombel/
Colorsport; pages 6, 7, top right, 9, 22, 25 top
and 29: Taillade/Colorsport; page 7 top left:
De Vries/Colorsport; pages 7 bottom and 25
bottom: Jumbo/Colorsport; pages 11, 23 and 26
right: Colorsport; page 13: Sellinger/
Colorsport pages 15 and 19: Compoint/
Colorsport; page 16: Tavernier/Colorsport;
page 21: Klein/Colorsport; page 26 left:
Maindru/Colorsport; page 27 top: Prior/
Colorsport; page 27 bottom: J. Allan Cash
Photo Library; page 28 all: Motor Group
Archives/Haymarket Publishing.

PRINTED IN BELGIUM BY

proost
INTERNATIONAL BOOK PRODUCTION